The Department of Education

KNOW YOUR GOVERNMENT

The Department of Education

Stephen J. Sniegoski

CHELSEA HOUSE PUBLISHERS

Editor-in-Chief: Nancy Toff
Executive Editor: Remmel T. Nunn
Managing Editor: Karyn Gullen Browne
Copy Chief: Juliann Barbato
Picture Editor: Adrian G. Allen
Art Director: Giannella Garrett
Manufacturing Manager: Gerald Levine

Staff for THE DEPARTMENT OF EDUCATION

Senior Editor: Elizabeth L. Mauro
Associate Editor: Pierre Hauser
Copyeditor: Michael Goodman
Editorial Assistant: Tara P. Deal
Picture Research: Domenico G. Firmani Associates, Inc.
Designer: Noreen M. Lamb
Layout: Foulk Purvis Design
Production Coordinator: Joseph Romano

Creative Director: Harold Steinberg

Library of Congress Cataloging-in-Publication Data

Sniegoski, Stephen J.
  The Department of Education.
  (Know your government)
  Bibliography: p.
  Includes index.
  1. United States. Dept. of Education—History.
2. Education and state—United States—History.
I. Title
LA210.S58 1987   379.73   87-8059
ISBN 0-87754-838-2

This manuscript was written by Stephen J. Sniegoski in his private capacity.
No official endorsement by the U.S. Department of Education is intended or
should be inferred.

CONTENTS

KNOW YOUR GOVERNMENT

THE AMERICAN RED CROSS

THE BUREAU OF INDIAN AFFAIRS

THE CENTRAL INTELLIGENCE AGENCY

THE COMMISSION ON CIVIL RIGHTS

THE DEPARTMENT OF AGRICULTURE

THE DEPARTMENT OF THE AIR FORCE

THE DEPARTMENT OF THE ARMY

THE DEPARTMENT OF COMMERCE

THE DEPARTMENT OF DEFENSE

THE DEPARTMENT OF EDUCATION

THE DEPARTMENT OF ENERGY

THE DEPARTMENT OF HEALTH AND
HUMAN SERVICES

THE DEPARTMENT OF HOUSING AND
URBAN DEVELOPMENT

THE DEPARTMENT OF THE INTERIOR

THE DEPARTMENT OF JUSTICE

THE DEPARTMENT OF LABOR

THE DEPARTMENT OF THE NAVY

THE DEPARTMENT OF STATE

THE DEPARTMENT OF TRANSPORTATION

THE DEPARTMENT OF THE TREASURY

THE DRUG ENFORCEMENT
ADMINISTRATION

THE ENVIRONMENTAL PROTECTION
AGENCY

THE EQUAL EMPLOYMENT
OPPORTUNITIES COMMISSION

THE FEDERAL AVIATION
ADMINISTRATION

THE FEDERAL BUREAU OF
INVESTIGATION

THE FEDERAL COMMUNICATIONS
COMMISSION

THE FEDERAL GOVERNMENT:
HOW IT WORKS

THE FEDERAL RESERVE SYSTEM

THE FEDERAL TRADE COMMISSION

THE FOOD AND DRUG ADMINISTRATION

THE FOREST SERVICE

THE HOUSE OF REPRESENTATIVES

THE IMMIGRATION AND
NATURALIZATION SERVICE

THE INTERNAL REVENUE SERVICE

THE LIBRARY OF CONGRESS

THE NATIONAL AERONAUTICS AND
SPACE ADMINISTRATION

THE NATIONAL ARCHIVES AND
RECORDS ADMINISTRATION

THE NATIONAL FOUNDATION ON
THE ARTS AND HUMANITIES

THE NATIONAL PARK SERVICE

THE NATIONAL SCIENCE FOUNDATION

THE NUCLEAR REGULATORY COMMISSION

THE PEACE CORPS

THE PRESIDENCY

THE PUBLIC HEALTH SERVICE

THE SECURITIES AND
EXCHANGE COMMISSION

THE SENATE

THE SMALL BUSINESS
ADMINISTRATION

THE SMITHSONIAN

THE SUPREME COURT

THE TENNESSEE VALLEY AUTHORITY

THE U.S. ARMS CONTROL AND
DISARMAMENT AGENCY

THE U.S. COAST GUARD

THE U.S. CONSTITUTION

THE U.S. FISH AND WILDLIFE SERVICE

THE U.S. INFORMATION AGENCY

THE U.S. MARINE CORPS

THE U.S. MINT

THE U.S. POSTAL SERVICE

THE U.S. SECRET SERVICE

THE VETERANS ADMINISTRATION

CHELSEA HOUSE PUBLISHERS

INTRODUCTION

Government: Crises of Confidence

Arthur M. Schlesinger, jr.

From the start, Americans have regarded their government with a mixture of reliance and mistrust. The men who founded the republic did not doubt the indispensability of government. "If men were angels," observed the 51st Federalist Paper, "no government would be necessary." But men are not angels. Since human beings are subject to wicked as well as to noble impulses, government was deemed essential to assure freedom and order.

At the same time, the American revolutionaries knew that government could also become a source of injury and oppression. The men who gathered in Philadelphia in 1787 to write the Constitution therefore had two purposes in mind. They wanted to establish a strong central authority and to limit that central authority's capacity to abuse its power.

To prevent the abuse of power, the founding fathers wrote two basic principles into the new Constitution. The principle of federalism divided power between the state governments and the central authority. The principle of the separation of powers subdivided the central authority itself into three branches—the executive, the legislative, and the judiciary—so that "each may be a check on the other." The *Know Your Government* series focuses on the major executive departments and agencies in these branches of the federal government.

The Constitution did not plan the executive branch in any detail. After vesting the executive power in the president, it assumed the existence of "executive departments" without specifying what these departments should be. Congress began defining their functions in 1789 by creating the Departments of State, Treasury, and War. The secretaries in charge of these departments made up President Washington's first cabinet. Congress also provided for a legal officer, and President Washington soon invited the attorney general, as he was called, to attend cabinet meetings. As need required, Congress created more executive departments.

Setting up the cabinet was only the first step in organizing the American state. With almost no guidance from the Constitution, President Washington, seconded by Alexander Hamilton, his brilliant secretary of the treasury, equipped the infant republic with a working administrative structure. The Federalists believed in both executive energy and executive accountability and set high standards for public appointments. The Jeffersonian opposition had less faith in strong government and preferred local government to the central authority. But when Jefferson himself became president in 1801, although he set out to change the direction of policy, he found no reason to alter the framework the Federalists had erected.

By 1801 there were about 3,000 federal civilian employees in a nation of a little more than 5 million people. Growth in territory and population steadily enlarged national responsibilities. Thirty years later, when Jackson was president, there were more than 11,000 government workers in a nation of 13 million.

The federal establishment was increasing at a faster rate than the population.

Jackson's presidency brought significant changes in the federal service. He believed that the executive branch contained too many officials who saw their jobs as "species of property" and as "a means of promoting individual interest." Against the idea of a permanent service based on life tenure, Jackson argued for the periodic redistribution of federal offices, contending that this was the democratic way and that official duties could be made "so plain and simple that men of intelligence may readily qualify themselves for their performance." He called this policy rotation-in-office. His opponents called it the spoils system.

In fact, partisan legend exaggerated the extent of Jackson's removals. More than 80 percent of federal officeholders retained their jobs. Jackson discharged no larger a proportion of government workers than Jefferson had done a generation earlier. But the rise in these years of mass political parties gave federal patronage new importance as a means of building the party and of rewarding activists. Jackson's successors were less restrained in the distribution of spoils. As the federal establishment grew—to nearly 40,000 by 1861—the politicization of the public service excited increasing concern.

After the Civil War the spoils system became a major political issue. High-minded men condemned it as the root of all political evil. The spoilsmen, said the British commentator James Bryce, "have distorted and depraved the mechanism of politics." Patronage, by giving jobs to unqualified, incompetent, and dishonest persons, lowered the standards of public service and nourished corrupt political machines. Office-seekers pursued presidents and cabinet secretaries without mercy. "Patronage," said Ulysses S. Grant after his presidency, "is the bane of the presidential office." "Every time I appoint someone to office," said another political leader, "I make a hundred enemies

9

and one ingrate." George William Curtis, the president of the National Civil Service Reform League, summed up the indictment. He said,

> The theory which perverts public trusts into party spoils, making public employment dependent upon personal favor and not on proved merit, necessarily ruins the self-respect of public employees, destroys the function of party in a republic, prostitutes elections into a desperate strife for personal profit, and degrades the national character by lowering the moral tone and standard of the country.

The object of civil service reform was to promote efficiency and honesty in the public service and to bring about the ethical regeneration of public life. Over bitter opposition from politicians, the reformers in 1883 passed the Pendleton Act, establishing a bipartisan Civil Service Commission, competitive examinations, and appointment on merit. The Pendleton Act also gave the president authority to extend by executive order the number of "classified" jobs—that is, jobs subject to the merit system. The act applied initially only to about 14,000 of the more than 100,000 federal positions. But by the end of the 19th century 40 percent of federal jobs had moved into the classified category.

Civil service reform was in part a response to the growing complexity of American life. As society grew more organized and problems more technical, official duties were no longer so plain and simple that any person of intelligence could perform them. In public service, as in other areas, the all-round man was yielding ground to the expert, the amateur to the professional. The excesses of the spoils system thus provoked the counter-ideal of scientific public administration, separate from politics and, as far as possible, insulated against it.

The cult of the expert, however, had its own excesses. The idea that administration could be divorced from policy was an illusion. And in the realm of policy, the expert, however much segregated from partisan politics, can never attain perfect objectivity. He remains the prisoner of his own set of values. It is these values rather than technical expertise that determine fundamental judgments of public policy. To turn over such judgments to experts, moreover, would be to abandon democracy itself; for in a democracy final decisions must be made by the people and their elected representatives. "The business of the expert," the British political scientist Harold Laski rightly said, "is to be on tap and not on top."

Politics, however, were deeply ingrained in American folkways. This meant intermittent tension between the presidential government, elected every four years by the people, and the permanent government, which saw presidents come and go while it went on forever. Sometimes the permanent government knew better than its political masters; sometimes it opposed or sabotaged valuable new initiatives. In the end a strong president with effective cabinet secretaries could make the permanent government responsive to presidential purpose, but it was often an exasperating struggle.

The struggle within the executive branch was less important, however, than the growing impatience with bureaucracy in society as a whole. The 20th century saw a considerable expansion of the federal establishment. The Great Depression and the New Deal led the national government to take on a variety of new responsibilities. The New Deal extended the federal regulatory apparatus. By 1940, in a nation of 130 million people, the number of federal workers for the first time passed the 1 million mark. The Second World War brought federal civilian employment to 3.8 million in 1945. With peace, the federal establishment declined to around 2 million by 1950. Then growth resumed, reaching 2.8 million by the 1980s.

The New Deal years saw rising criticism of "big government" and "bureaucracy." Businessmen resented federal regulation. Conservatives worried about the impact of paternalistic government on individual self-reliance, on community responsibility, and on economic and personal freedom. The nation in effect renewed the old debate between Hamilton and Jefferson in the early republic, although with an ironic exchange of positions. For the Hamiltonian constituency, the "rich and well-born," once the advocate of affirmative government, now condemned government intervention, while the Jeffersonian constituency, the plain people, once the advocate of a weak central government and of states' rights, now favored government intervention.

In the 1980s, with the presidency of Ronald Reagan, the debate has burst out with unusual intensity. According to conservatives, government intervention abridges liberty, stifles enterprise, and is inefficient, wasteful, and arbitrary. It disturbs the harmony of the self-adjusting market and creates worse troubles than it solves. Get government off our backs, according to the popular cliché, and our problems will solve themselves. When government is necessary, let it be at the local level, close to the people. Above all, stop the inexorable growth of the federal government.

In fact, for all the talk about the "swollen" and "bloated" bureaucracy, the federal establishment has not been growing as inexorably as many Americans seem to believe. In 1949, it consisted of 2.1 million people. Thirty years later, while the country had grown by 70 million, the federal force had grown only by 750,000. Federal workers were a smaller percentage of the population in 1985 than they were in 1955—or in 1940. The federal establishment, in short, has not kept pace with population growth. Moreover, national defense and the postal service account for 60 percent of federal employment.

Why then the widespread idea about the remorseless growth of government? It is partly because in the 1960s the national government assumed new and intrusive functions:

affirmative action in civil rights, environmental protection, safety and health in the workplace, community organization, legal aid to the poor. Although this enlargement of the federal regulatory role was accompanied by marked growth in the size of government on all levels, the expansion has taken place primarily in state and local government. Whereas the federal force increased by only 27 percent in the 30 years after 1950, the state and local government force increased by an astonishing 212 percent.

Despite the statistics, the conviction flourishes in some minds that the national government is a steadily growing behemoth swallowing up the liberties of the people. The foes of Washington prefer local government, feeling it is closer to the people and therefore allegedly more responsive to popular needs. Obviously there is a great deal to be said for settling local questions locally. But local government is characteristically the government of the locally powerful. Historically, the way the locally powerless have won their human and constitutional rights has often been through appeal to the national government. The national government has vindicated racial justice against local bigotry, defended the Bill of Rights against local vigilantism, and protected natural resources against local greed. It has civilized industry and secured the rights of labor organizations. Had the states' rights creed prevailed, there would perhaps still be slavery in the United States.

The national authority, far from diminishing the individual, has given most Americans more personal dignity and liberty than ever before. The individual freedoms destroyed by the increase in national authority have been in the main the freedom to deny black Americans their rights as citizens; the freedom to put small children to work in mills and immigrants in sweatshops; the freedom to pay starvation wages, require barbarous working hours, and permit squalid working conditions; the freedom to deceive in the sale of goods and securities; the

13

freedom to pollute the environment—all freedoms that, one supposes, a civilized nation can readily do without.

"Statements are made," said President John F. Kennedy in 1963, "labelling the Federal Government an outsider, an intruder, an adversary.... The United States Government is not a stranger or not an enemy. It is the people of fifty states joining in a national effort.... Only a great national effort by a great people working together can explore the mysteries of space, harvest the products at the bottom of the ocean, and mobilize the human, natural, and material resources of our lands."

So an old debate continues. However, Americans are of two minds. When pollsters ask large, spacious questions—Do you think government has become too involved in your lives? Do you think government should stop regulating business?—a sizable majority opposes big government. But when asked specific questions about the practical work of government—Do you favor social security? unemployment compensation? Medicare? health and safety standards in factories? environmental protection? government guarantee of jobs for everyone seeking employment? price and wage controls when inflation threatens?—a sizable majority approves of intervention.

In general, Americans do not want less government. What they want is more efficient government. They want government to do a better job. For a time in the 1970s, with Vietnam and Watergate, Americans lost confidence in the national government. In 1964, more than three-quarters of those polled had thought the national government could be trusted to do right most of the time. By 1980 only one-quarter was prepared to offer such trust. But by 1984 trust in the federal government to manage national affairs had climbed back to 45 percent.

Bureaucracy is a term of abuse. But it is impossible to run any large organization, whether public or private, without a bureaucracy's division of labor and hierarchy of authority. And we live in a world of large organizations. Without bureaucracy modern society would collapse. The problem is not to abolish bureaucracy, but to make it flexible, efficient, and capable of innovation.

Two hundred years after the drafting of the Constitution, Americans still regard government with a mixture of reliance and mistrust—a good combination. Mistrust is the best way to keep government reliable. Informed criticism is the means of correcting governmental inefficiency, incompetence, and arbitrariness; that is, of best enabling government to play its essential role. For without government, we cannot attain the goals of the founding fathers. Without an understanding of government, we cannot have the informed criticism that makes government do the job right. It is the duty of every American citizen to *Know Your Government*—which is what this series is all about.

The Department of Education attempts to improve the quality of American education by conducting educational research, providing financial aid to local school boards, and developing innovative programs such as bilingual instruction.

ONE

Education in America

In many countries, the federal government completely controls academic life. Education ministries determine public school curricula (educational programs) and college admission standards. Some countries even use quota systems to determine how many people can attend school and what they can study. But in the United States, the federal government has little control over education. Although it can recommend measures to improve public schools, it cannot enact these recommendations. That type of educational authority rests with states, localities, and private institutions.

Nevertheless, the United States Department of Education plays an important role in American education. As the nation's leading educational researcher, it spots educational trends, surveys teaching techniques, and decides what works—and what does not—in America's schools. And, although it has no direct authority over school policy, it has the power to distribute federal education funds. Along with this power comes the right to deny funds to schools that do not comply with educational requirements legislated by Congress.

Furthermore, as a cabinet-level agency, the department has the power of the presidency behind it. The secretary of education is the president's chief education advisor and spokesperson. The secretary's policies reflect the president's priorities and concerns. This presidential authority gives the secretary great influence over schools and educators.

But presidential influence goes only so far, because most Americans have strong opinions about education. Differing views on what should be taught—and how—have sparked debate throughout the nation's history. In the early days of the nation, many people objected to any federal role in public education. In recent years, people have reacted strongly—sometimes violently—to programs such as sex education and racial desegregation. In some areas of the country, educators, legislators, and citizens still debate these issues, along with other controversial subjects, such as school prayer, bilingual education, and the teaching of the theory of evolution.

The emotional nature of these arguments has often silenced the federal government. In many cases, the government has left decisions on such controversial issues to state and local authorities who formulate school curricula and policy for their areas. Yet, when local practices violate federal laws (as in the case of segregation) the Department of Education has used its power to grant or deny education funds. And this has often forced local authorities to obey those federal laws.

In recent years, the department has turned its attention to the decline in American academic achievement. Studies show that American students consistently lag behind students from other nations in standardized test scores. Despite opposition from those who think the federal government should stay out of the nation's schools, the Department of Education is leading the fight to reestablish American scholarship.

A Maine teacher displays books banned from the classroom by her school's English department, over the objections of several parents. State and local authorities retain the power to set curricula for American schools.

Today, many innovative programs in American schools, colleges, and universities derive from the department's research and development efforts. Its research has revealed America's educational needs, its scholars and philosophers have recommended remedies, and its administration has granted funds to improve education. Furthermore, thousands of American educators rely on the department's many publications to keep them abreast of the latest educational trends and techniques.

Although today's Department of Education was not created until 1979, the Federal government has been involved in education since the nation's beginning. And since then, the government has tried to reconcile the need for national education policy with the American love of liberty and freedom in daily life. Maintaining this balance continues to be the department's greatest challenge.

Many of the nation's founding fathers, including Benjamin Franklin, believed that the federal government should play a major role in formulating educational policy.

TWO

The Department's Beginnings

Americans have always valued education. The leaders who created the nation's first laws gave considerable thought to the government's role in educational policy. George Washington wanted to create a national university, and Benjamin Franklin formed the American Philosophical Society, which later offered a prize "for the best system of liberal education and literary instruction, adapted to the genius of the United States."

Thomas Jefferson believed that education was necessary to the very survival of democracy. "If a nation expects to be both ignorant and free," he said, "it expects what never was and never will be." Jefferson even proposed that the federal government bring the University of Geneva's faculty to the United States to provide quality education to young Americans.

Although nothing resulted from most of these visionary schemes, they reflected a national esteem for education that has influenced federal policy since the nation's birth. Washington,

Franklin, Jefferson, and others began working toward a national education policy even before the Constitution was written. In 1785, the Continental Congress enacted the Land Ordinance to set aside portions of public lands in the Northwest Territory for schools. And in the Northwest Ordinance of 1787, Congress decreed that "schools and the means of education shall forever be encouraged" in that territory.

Convinced that a strong educational system was vital in a democracy, Thomas Jefferson urged the federal government to import scholars from European universities.

In colonial times, most Americans received their primary and secondary educations in one-room schoolhouses operated by churches and community groups.

Nevertheless, when the United States Constitution was drafted in late 1787, it made no mention of education. Many Americans were suspicious of too much federal control over their lives, and most thought education was the responsibility of families, churches, and charitable groups. So the Constitution's framers decided to promote education in subtle ways without making specific provisions in the Constitution.

After the Constitution's ratification, the federal government passed many laws promoting education. In the early 1800s, Congress gave land grants to specific state and private educational institutions and required states to devote some of the proceeds from public land sales to education. Yet, the federal role in public education remained limited because the Constitution did not specifically empower the federal government to enact an education policy—and because the Bill of Rights stated that "the powers not delegated to the United States by the Constitution . . . are reserved to the States."

A 19th-century engraving shows pupils walking home from their schoolhouse. In the early 1800s, Congress promoted learning by donating federal land to schools and requiring states to allocate a percentage of revenues to education.

The absence of federal supervision resulted in an uneven and fragmented educational structure. Soon, educators began to question the lack of uniformity in American education. By the mid-1800s, a public school movement was underway across the country. Many northern states established public schools and created centralized education departments to collect educational data and provide the schools with some direction. The success of these state agencies prompted many educators to push for a federal department to perform similar functions for the nation.

Soon, America's leading educators offered proposals for a national education agency. One of the foremost proponents of such an agency was Henry Barnard, a graduate of Yale College (now Yale University) and editor of *The American Journal of Education*. Barnard had gained acclaim among American educators by standardizing public schools in Connecticut and Rhode Island.

On a trip across the country, Barnard noted a lack of standardized educational information. Believing that information was the key to educational success, Barnard began campaigning for a national education office.

Barnard's reputation helped him gain widespread support among his fellow educators, but convincing the federal government was difficult. Although he persuaded officials to include education questions in the United States census, Barnard was unable to convince the government to expand its educational role.

A prominent northeastern educator, Henry Barnard led the fight to create a national education department and in 1867 became its first commissioner.

The Department of Education Bill

In the 1860s, the national mood toward education began to change. After the Civil War, federal involvement in daily life increased, conditioning many Americans to accept federal involvement in education. Furthermore, most opposition to a stronger federal role in education had originated in the South, which after the war was too weak and fragmented to protest.

This shift in attitude emboldened proponents of a federal education agency. In February 1866, the National Association of School Superintendents—which strongly supported Barnard's efforts—asked Congress to establish a federal bureau of education. Congressman James A. Garfield of Ohio (who later became president) presented the request to the House of Representatives. The House passed the bill and sent it to the Senate for approval.

On February 28, 1867, the Senate approved a bill to establish an autonomous, non-cabinet-level Department of Education. But obtaining President Andrew Johnson's signature promised to be difficult. Johnson believed that the states held the right to control their internal affairs. Fearing an expansion of federal power into the states' domain, the president intended to veto the Department of Education bill.

But Senator James Dixon of Connecticut persuaded Johnson not to exercise his veto. Dixon, one of the president's few Republican supporters in Congress and a close friend of Henry Barnard, urged the president to approve the bill. On March 2, 1867, Johnson signed the bill giving birth to the Department of Education.

The Department of Education bill required the new agency to collect and distribute facts and figures on the management, organization, and teaching methods of the nation's schools. This information, the bill declared, "shall aid the people of the United States in the establishment and maintenance of efficient school systems, and otherwise promote the cause of education through-

On March 2, 1867, President Andrew Johnson signed into law a bill establishing the Department of Education. In its initial form, the department was a noncabinet-level agency responsible primarily for research.

out the country." Although the task of promoting education throughout the country implied broad powers, the department had no authority to establish a national system of education. It could only provide information to the states and hope that they would use it to promote education.

An 1881 sketch of a Boston kindergarten. In its early years, the Education Department devoted its limited resources to assessing the condition of the nation's schools.

Furthermore, in an age of small government agencies and limited budgets, the education department had a staff of only three clerks and a total budget of just $15,000. With these meager resources, the department was expected to collect statistics that were virtually nonexistent in the southern states and largely inaccurate and incomplete in the northern states. The task was enormous.

Commissioner Barnard

President Johnson needed someone exceptional to run the new department. He chose Barnard, the man who was most responsible for the department's existence. Although Barnard was one of America's leading educators, he was poorly suited to such a taxing administrative job.

A loner, Barnard neglected political concerns and refused to ingratiate himself with Congress. He did not complete his 1867 annual report to Congress until the summer of 1868. So for more than a year, the department had nothing to show for its efforts. When he finally presented the report, practical-minded members of Congress found its 900 pages of statistics on illiteracy, the legal status of black students, and courses of study too abstract. Moreover, Barnard's ill health forced him to spend most of his time away from Washington, and he soon lost touch with his own staff. The department's image suffered.

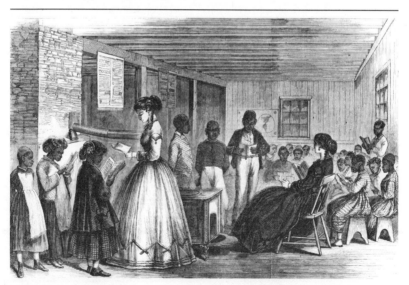

An 1866 engraving of an all-black school in Virginia. In Henry Barnard's first annual report to Congress, he addressed the legal status of black students.

Edward D. Neill, the department's chief clerk, added to Barnard's woes. A Minnesota educator and a personal secretary to Presidents Lincoln and Johnson, Neill felt that the president should have appointed him as department commissioner. He resented his role as a clerk and frequently spoke ill of Barnard to his friends in Congress and the White House. After Barnard fired him in December 1867, Neill continued to criticize the department and its commissioner.

Neill's criticism and Barnard's inefficiency caused growing opposition to the department. Many members of Congress who had supported its creation turned against it. At a time when Congress wanted to cut federal spending, it targeted the seemingly worthless Department of Education for economizing.

On July 20, 1868, Congress reduced the department's budget for the next year's operations to about $9,000. It also

Interior Secretary Orville Browning sought unsuccessfully to disband the Department of Education after it was renamed the Office of Education and made a branch of his department in 1869.

decided that on June 30, 1869, the Department of Education would become the Office of Education, a branch of the Department of the Interior. Congress made this decision even though Interior Secretary Orville H. Browning thought the Department of Education should be abolished and had publicly stated that there was "no necessity of knowing anything whatever about education." (Fortunately for the agency, Browning left office in 1869.)

In 1870, Congress again sought to limit the agency's role. It changed the Office of Education's name to the Bureau of Education and cut its budget to just $5,000. Many people blamed Congress's actions on Barnard's poor management, and on March 15, 1870, he resigned. Ironically, the man who had worked to establish the national education agency had nearly caused its elimination.

In the late 1800s, the nation's educational system flourished. Here, students receive instruction at a school for the deaf.

THREE

A New Emphasis
on Education

As 1870 drew to a close, the Bureau of Education seemed to have lost its authority to promote education throughout the country. It also looked as if education concerns would be neglected by the secretary of the interior, who now had control over the bureau. But the bureau soon found that as part of a large, cabinet-level department, it enjoyed considerable independence in its everyday affairs.

The first person to enjoy this freedom was John Eaton, appointed by President Ulysses S. Grant to succeed Barnard as commissioner of education. Eaton, a Union general who had led an all-black platoon during the Civil War, had been a high-ranking official in the Freedman's Bureau, a federal program established to help freed slaves adjust to their new lives. Before becoming commissioner, Eaton had taught school in New Hampshire and had been Tennessee's superintendent of schools.

Eaton brought a fresh approach to the bureau. He visited the nation's schools and worked closely with educational organi-

Commissioner John Eaton convinced Congress to look more favorably at the Bureau of Education (as the office was renamed in 1870).

zations such as the National Education Association (NEA), a teachers' group. An able administrator with political savvy, Eaton established friendly relations with Congress. Soon, Congress allowed him to expand his staff and make improvements. Eaton enlarged and cataloged the agency's library and established an education museum. When Eaton left office in 1886, the bureau's budget had grown to $100,000, and its staff to 38.

President Grover Cleveland appointed H. R. Dawson as Eaton's successor. Dawson was an attorney and politician whose only experience in education was as a trustee of the University of Alabama. Nevertheless, he managed the department well, streamlining its operations and promoting its educational publications.

Under Commissioner Harris

Dawson left the bureau in 1889, when President Cleveland's first term expired. The bureau's next commissioner, William Torrey Harris, was appointed by President Benjamin Harrison and continued to serve under the following three presidents. A noted educator, Harris emphasized traditional academics. He strongly opposed the emerging "progressive" education movement, which highlighted such curricula as home economics, health, vocational education, and citizenship. Although this movement would dominate the thinking of 20th-century American educators, Harris fended it off during his term.

As commissioner of the Education Bureau from 1899 to 1911, William Harris presided over two major programs, one that gave the states land grants for colleges and another that provided Alaskan Eskimos with educational facilities and financial assistance.

As one facet of the Alaskan Program, Education Bureau representatives taught Eskimos how to herd reindeer.

During Harris's tenure, one of the bureau's major responsibilities was the administration of the second Morrill Land Grant Act. This act provided states with federal grants of land for agricultural and industrial colleges. These grants helped establish dozens of schools throughout the country. But the bureau's most intriguing program during Harris's term involved reindeer herding in Alaska.

Since 1885, the Bureau of Education had been in charge of the Alaska Program, which involved operating schools in Alaska as well as delivering medical supplies and ensuring the economic well-being of the native Alaskans, or Eskimos. In 1890, the bureau's general agent in Alaska, Sheldon Jackson, reported that commercial hunters were killing the whales, seals, and walruses that the Eskimos needed for food. Jackson suggested that the Eskimos could once again provide for themselves if they were introduced to reindeer herding.

Since the bureau's responsibilities included ensuring the Eskimos' economic well-being, Commissioner Harris ardently supported the plan. When Congress refused to fund the project, the bureau used private donations to purchase Siberian reindeer and to hire herders to teach the Eskimos their craft. The plan enjoyed such success that in 1893, Congress began to provide financial support for the project.

In addition to administering these programs, Harris used his position as head of the bureau to promote his educational views. His many articles and lectures advanced the bureau's intellectual prestige. But because Harris was largely indifferent to administrative detail, the day-to-day operations of the bureau suffered during his term.

Claxton and World War I

In 1911, President William Howard Taft appointed P. P. Claxton as commissioner of education. During Claxton's term, the out-

Under P. P. Claxton, education commissioner during World War I, the bureau enlarged its budget and developed new programs, such as vocational training.

break of World War I caused the bureau to grow significantly. In 1920, the bureau's budget (excluding the Alaska Program) exceeded $500,000—more than four times the 1910 figure.

New wartime programs accounted for most of this increase. They included such things as technical training to aid wartime industries, civics programs to help immigrants join the American mainstream, and the United States Garden Army Project, which encouraged students to cultivate school yards and other areas to provide food for the war effort. Other types of projects also began during Claxton's tenure. For example, the bureau created programs to study issues related to kindergarten education, black education, and industrial, agricultural, and commercial training.

Students tend crops in their school yard as part of an Education Bureau project for augmenting American food supplies during World War I.

Schoolchildren receive lunches from workers for the Red Cross, one of several agencies that supplemented Education Bureau efforts during the 1920s.

When Warren G. Harding became president in 1921, he replaced Claxton with John James Tigert, a former Rhodes scholar and all-American football player. Tigert, who also served under President Calvin Coolidge, could not expand the bureau because Congress was looking for ways to cut government spending.

A Shift in Focus

In 1929, William John Cooper replaced Tigert as commissioner. Cooper believed that the bureau should focus on educational research and data gathering. He also felt that it should stop administering non-educational projects such as the Alaska Program. Consequently, the reindeer program was transferred to the Bureau of Indian Affairs (BIA) in 1929. (The BIA took over the rest of the Alaska Program, including school operation, in 1931.)

To emphasize the renewed focus on research, the bureau once again changed its name. In 1929, it resumed the title Office of Education, because many felt the term "office" implied a specialized emphasis. Over the next few years, the office lived up to its name by undertaking a number of new educational surveys.

The most important education issue during Cooper's term arose in the early 1930s, in response to a report from the National Advisory Committee on Education. (President Hoover had created the committee, an independent panel of education experts, to study educational concerns.) The committee recommended that the government's many educational activities be consolidated in a single, cabinet-level Department of Education. It also called for general federal aid to education (aid that states could use for day-to-day educational activities).

An American train carries weapons through France during World War I. One of the Education Bureau's wartime projects involved training civilians to work in munitions plants.

The time seemed right for these drastic changes in the federal education role. During World War I, Americans had become acutely aware of deficiencies in the nation's educational system when they learned that many soldiers were illiterate. Throughout the 1920s, legislators had proposed dozens of measures to improve education. Unfortunately, the Great Depression devastated the nation's economy and stalled attempts to implement the committee's recommendations.

The New Deal and World War II

The depression almost destroyed the entire federal education effort. To cope with the dramatic decrease in federal tax revenues, Congress severely pared government expenditures. In 1932, the Office of Education suffered massive funding cuts and laid off many staff members or placed them on part-time schedules. The crisis was so severe that Commissioner Cooper had to use private funds to complete his final education survey.

In 1933, Franklin D. Roosevelt became president. He ushered in the New Deal, a slate of federally funded programs designed to provide economic aid for Americans affected by the depression. Many educators hoped that the New Deal would increase federal participation in education. But when Roosevelt established youth programs that emphasized vocational training, some educators feared that he was creating a system that would compete with the established educational structure.

Such fears were exaggerated. Many New Deal programs actually aided traditional education. Under Commissioner John Ward Studebaker, the Office of Education took charge of education for one New Deal program, the Civilian Conservation Corps, and helped operate education programs for another, the National Youth Administration. And the New Deal's Works Progress Administration provided money to help states and localities operate schools that suffered from diminished tax revenues.

During the 1930s, the Office of Education also developed educational programs for radio. In the mid-1930s, democracy seemed threatened by fascism and communism, movements that were dominating Europe. Commissioner Studebaker believed that radio could promote democratic values. Although the project never made significant headway, it received great publicity.

A worker for the Works Progress Administration—one of several New Deal programs that offered vocational instruction—shows a student how to cut steel with an acetylene torch.

John Studebaker directed the Office of Education (as the bureau was renamed in 1929) during the New Deal and World War II.

When the United States entered World War II in 1941, the Office of Education expanded dramatically—although temporarily. It helped train thousands of Americans for work in wartime industries. By 1945, the Office of Education administered more than $81 million in grants with a staff of almost 500 employees. Although Commissioner Studebaker wanted this increase to be permanent, cutbacks after the war reduced the staff to 286 in 1947.

Gifted pupils type their lessons at a New York City school. During the 1950s, the Education Office, as part of its new activism, developed many programs for exceptional students.

FOUR

The Onset of Federal Activism

At the end of the 1940s, the Office of Education still closely resembled the department founded in 1867. Despite numerous name changes and dozens of new programs, its duties remained what they had been from the beginning: gathering and disseminating information. But the onset of the 1950s ushered in a period of tremendous political and social change in the United States. Over the next three decades, the Office of Education would change dramatically.

The federal government became committed to centralizing authority for American education. But states and localities had considerable control over their schools, and the federal government had few means of implementing its policies. To help the government promote change, Congress enacted numerous aid-to-education programs for the Office of Education to administer.

Ostensibly, the purpose of these programs was to provide aid to local school districts. But their real purpose was to give the federal government a way of forcing schools to comply with federal legislation. To accomplish this, Congress gave the Office of Education the power of the purse—the authority to distribute federal funds to schools. The Office of Education required schools to prove compliance with federal laws before they could receive funding. It also wrote regulations enforcing federal laws and monitored adherence to these regulations. If state or local education authorities did not comply with the office's guidelines, the office could cut off federal funds.

Several acts also helped the Office of Education implement its new agenda. In 1953, it became part of the new Department of Health, Education and Welfare (HEW). The following year, Congress passed the Cooperative Research Act, which gave the office the power to stimulate educational research with grants to colleges and universities. And in 1958, in response to Soviet technological achievements such as the launch of the first artificial satellite, Congress enacted the National Defense Education Act. This law mandated federal aid to education in mathematics, science, and foreign languages.

The Soviet Union's 1957 launching of Sputnik I, the first earth satellite, convinced American leaders that the United States was losing the space race and prompted a nationwide campaign to improve education in the sciences.

Johnson's War on Poverty

By 1960, new programs had increased the Office of Education's staff to almost 1,100 people and its budget to more than $400 million. But its greatest expansion occurred in 1964, when President Lyndon B. Johnson inaugurated his War on Poverty programs to help the poor and disadvantaged.

President Johnson believed that poor educational achievement was the major cause of poverty in America. Through education, Johnson believed, the poor could move into the middle class. Therefore, in 1964 Johnson proposed legislation to aid disadvantaged students from elementary school through college. Congress turned his proposals into law by passing the Elementary and Secondary Education Act and the Higher Education Act.

After their passage in 1965, these two acts greatly expanded the Office of Education. Its budget skyrocketed from $1.5 billion in 1965 to $3.4 billion in 1966, and its staff grew from 2,113 to 3,198. Furthermore, the office's structure and emphasis

In 1965, President Lyndon Johnson won approval of two major bills providing aid to disadvantaged students. Abandoning its focus on research, the Education Office administered the new programs.

changed. It was transformed from a collection of researchers who issued specialized reports to an organization of managers who administered federal programs. Because educational research had been the office's traditional function, many believed that Johnson's program-oriented Office of Education was betraying the office's intended purpose.

Nixon and the NIE

President Richard M. Nixon, who took office in 1969, was one of those who felt that the Office of Education had strayed from its original purpose. Nixon emphasized government efficiency and economy rather than federally directed social change. He wanted to create a new educational research organization, staffed by social scientists, that would operate independently of the Office of Education.

Congress agreed, and so it passed the Education Amendments of 1972, a package of legislation that amended a number of previous education acts. The amendments transferred most educational research activities to the new National Institute of Education (NIE). (NIE and the Office of Education formed co-equal parts of a new Education Division of HEW.) Then, in 1974, Congress transferred the National Center for Education Statistics (NCES) from the Office of Education to the Office of HEW's assistant secretary for education. Thus, by the mid-1970s, Congress had removed from the Office of Education most functions not related to funding.

In the late 1960s and the 1970s, the government's education efforts focused on advancing the causes of racial minorities, women, and the handicapped—groups that had been denied equality in education. Previous programs had tried to integrate the disadvantaged into the American mainstream, but these new efforts attempted instead to alter the mainstream. Programs such as bilingual education (teaching non-English-speaking stu-

A girl demonstrates for her classmates that wet paper will not ignite. The Office of Civil Rights protects the rights of female students to study science and other traditionally male-dominated disciplines.

dents partially in their native language), and new teaching aids such as nonsexist textbooks, began to change traditional teaching methods.

The Office of Civil Rights

Many efforts to promote equality were directed by the Office of Civil Rights (OCR), an office within HEW that was responsible for enforcing laws against discrimination in federally assisted education programs. Controversy often surrounded the OCR's actions. Conservatives viewed them as social engineering, and many local and state school officials saw them as excessive federal intrusion.

One of the most controversial laws the OCR had to enforce was the Bilingual Education Act of 1968, which allowed the federal government to issue guidelines for bilingual education. Members of Congress, school officials, and many citizens protested. Many believed that these students should be taught to speak English and should then attend classes conducted in English. Nevertheless, bilingual education programs continued.

Another controversial OCR action involved an attempt to achieve racial balance in state universities in the south. Many of these schools remained segregated even after the Supreme Court declared the practice unconstitutional in 1954. The OCR sought to make predominantly white and predominantly black colleges offer courses to attract a multiracial student body. These demands caused considerable hostility from both white and black colleges. Many black schools protested that they wanted to maintain the racial identity of their institutions.

The OCR caused more controversy when it tried to combat educational discrimination against women. Under Title IX of the Higher Education Act of 1972, which prohibited discrimination on the basis of sex in federally funded educational programs, the OCR forced schools to allocate a greater portion of their budgets to womens' athletics.

Another attempt to protect women's rights in schools was the Women's Educational Equity Act, passed in 1974. The act provided grants to develop textbooks and curricula that encouraged women to enter traditionally male occupations.

Black student leaders at Harvard University in 1968. During the 1960s the Office of Civil Rights, which later joined the Education Department, pushed for integration of colleges.

High school field hockey players in Maryland. In 1972, the Education Department began using Title IX—a federal law forbidding sexual discrimination in education—to force schools to improve athletic programs for women.

Education Under Fire

Despite these efforts to improve education—or perhaps because of them—Americans severely criticized public education during the 1970s. Some of this criticism resulted from the public's general disenchantment with "big government" and high taxes. But education was singled out for criticism because of the apparent deterioration in academic achievement.

Between 1962 and 1980, Scholastic Aptitude Test (SAT) scores dropped from an average of 478 (of a possible 800) to only 424 for the verbal test and from 502 to 466 for the math test. American College Testing (ACT), another academic exam, experienced a similar decline in scores. Critics claimed that these declines coincided with the vast increase in federal involvement in education and that the emphasis on federal programs had forced schools to neglect traditional academics.

Despite this hostility, however, the federal government continued to increase its involvement in education. And in the late 1970s, many educators issued pleas for a stronger federal commitment to education.

51

Delegates from the National Educational Association (NEA), a teachers' union, cheer for Jimmy Carter at the 1976 Democratic convention. After becoming president, Carter rewarded the NEA for its support by creating a cabinet-level education department.

FIVE

The New Department of Education

Since the late 1800s, American educators had fought for a cabinet-level education agency. Again and again, they had proposed bills to establish such a department. President Hoover's National Advisory Committee on Education had called for an education department as early as the 1920s. In the 1960s, President Johnson had created three separate task forces to study the issue. In spite of these efforts, by the 1970s the nation still had no cabinet-level department of education.

Joining Carter's Cabinet

By the mid-1970s, the National Education Association (NEA), a teachers' union and lobbying group numbering 1.8 million members, had become one of the most powerful political organizations in the United States. When Jimmy Carter ran for president in 1976, he actively sought NEA support by promising to back the group's education program. As a result, the NEA agreed to do what it had never done before—endorse a presidential candidate and actively campaign for him.

Carter won the presidency by an extremely narrow margin, and NEA support helped him win it. Therefore, Carter felt obliged to address the primary issue of the NEA's education program—the establishment of a cabinet-level Department of Education. In April 1977, the Carter administration began studying this issue.

Proponents of a cabinet-level department argued that it would improve efficiency. It would eliminate the fragmentation and duplication of effort that existed within the Education Division of the Department of Health, Education and Welfare (HEW). They also claimed that creating a separate education department would enable an administrator with educational expertise to determine national education policy.

Critics—including such notables as HEW Secretary Joseph Califano—argued that the federal education structure could be reorganized without creating a new, cabinet-level department. They feared that the proposed department would be run by professional educators who would pursue their own interests. Even the American Federation of Teachers opposed the department, fearing it would be dominated by their rival organization, the NEA. And, as always, critics claimed that a cabinet-level department would inevitably result in too large a federal role in American education.

Congress held extensive hearings on the matter, weighing all viewpoints. In 1978, the Senate voted in favor of a bill to create a Department of Education. But a similar bill in the House of Representatives never made it to a vote, despite intense NEA lobbying. Nevertheless, President Carter revived the measure to create a Department of Education in 1979, when he launched an intense lobbying campaign.

Once again, the bill easily passed in the Senate but faced

Health, Education, and Welfare secretary Joseph Califano opposed the establishment of an education department, warning that it would be taken over by the teachers' lobby.

tough opposition in the House. This time, however, the House passed the bill by a slim margin. After ironing out the minor differences between the Senate and House versions of the bill, both houses of Congress passed the Department of Education bill in September 1979.

The final bill appeased opponents by reaffirming state and local control of education and by requiring a staff reduction for the new department. On October 17, 1979, President Carter signed the Department of Education Organization Act, making the department a cabinet-level agency at last.

Surrounded by supporters, President Carter prepares to sign the Department of Education Organization Act on October 17, 1979. The act created the cabinet-level Education Department.

The new Department of Education was composed primarily of the Education Division of HEW, which was renamed the Department of Health and Human Services. The National Institute of Education (NIE) and the National Center for Education Statistics (NCES) joined the Office of Educational Research and Improvement (OERI), one of the major offices of the department. The Office of Civil Rights (OCR), which had been part of the Office of the Secretary of HEW, also became part of the Department of Education.

To head the new Department of Education, President Carter selected Shirley M. Hufstedler, the highest-ranking female judge in the United States. The Senate confirmed her nomination and she became secretary of education on December 6, 1979. Hufstedler presided over a 180-day transition period established to allow for the department's organization. On May 4,

1980, the Department of Education officially opened its doors with Hufstedler at the helm.

The new department had barely begun operations when the 1980 presidential campaign began. During the campaign, Republican candidate Ronald Reagan called for the abolition of the Department of Education, siding with those who supported more localized control. President Carter, running for a second term, vowed to keep the new department going. But despite ardent NEA support, Carter lost the election. Reagan entered office pledging to abolish the department and greatly reduce federal participation in educational matters.

In 1979, President Carter chose Shirley M. Hufstedler, then the nation's highest-ranking woman judge, to head the new Department of Education.

Under the Reagan Administration

Reagan chose Terrel H. Bell, a longtime advocate of federal involvement in education, as the new secretary of education. As commissioner of education under Presidents Nixon and Ford, Bell had supported the department's creation. Now he echoed Reagan's call for dismantling the department.

Bell suggested that the department be transformed into a non-cabinet-level federal foundation for education assistance, but

Terrel Bell, President Reagan's first secretary of education, addresses a meeting of the American Federation of Teachers. Bell proposed changing the department into a federal foundation.

his proposal gained little support. Moderates and liberals who objected to the department's structure nevertheless supported a strong federal role in education. Conservatives who wanted fewer federal programs felt that Bell's proposal would do little to diminish the federal role.

This lack of support forced Reagan to give the department's abolition low priority during his first administration. Nevertheless, his administration managed to diminish the federal role in education. For instance, it convinced Congress to pass the Education Consolidation and Improvement Act of 1981, which gave state and local governments more authority in administering federal education funds.

The same year, Bell created the National Commission on Excellence in Education to investigate the widely publicized decline in national academic achievement. The commission's major report, *A Nation at Risk*, confirmed this dramatic decline and recommended a return to basic academic curricula. Bell de-emphasized controversial activities, such as bilingual education, and focused on programs with more popular support. For example, in response to the public's fascination with computers, Bell launched a program to study and promote the use of high technology in education.

Bell resigned his cabinet post in 1984, having decided that he no longer wished to support his department's agenda. To succeed Bell, Reagan chose William J. Bennett, who had been the chairman of the National Endowment for the Humanities during Reagan's first term. A former head of the private National Center for the Humanities, Bennett was a conservative Democrat who favored traditional education.

Bennett's educational agenda emphasized the "Three Cs"— content, character, and choice. He proposed that the content of public school curricula should stress traditional academics and liberal arts (literature and history, for example). Character, Bennett contended, was built by teaching students Judeo-Christian ideals, which he felt the public schools had neglected. Choice involved supporting tuition tax credits, tax breaks for those who chose to send their children to private schools. Bennett also advocated providing federal funds to allow the disadvantaged to attend private schools.

In March 1986, Bennett released a major educational report entitled *What Works*. Written for the public as well as for professional educators, the report emphasized traditional teaching methods, such as memorizing, phonetic reading, and homework assignments. The report also stressed discipline and parental involvement in education.

A boy studies grammar on a computer. Secretary Bell launched a campaign to encourage the use of advanced technology in the classroom.

A nun addresses her class. William Bennett, who became secretary of education in 1984, advocated tax breaks for parents of private school students.

Under the Reagan administration, the Department of Education actively promoted quality education for the nation. Although Reagan came into office pledging to disband the department in order to give state and local governments more educational control, this did not occur. However, some legislation, such as the Education Consolidation and Improvement Act, reduced federal involvement in education.

Located near the Capitol, Federal Office Building Number 6 serves as the Department of Education's headquarters.

SIX

Inside the
Department

By federal government standards, the Department of Education is small. Whereas the Department of Defense, the nation's largest cabinet-level agency, has a staff of more than one million employees and a budget of more than $258 billion, the Department of Education has fewer than 5,000 employees and an annual budget of about $18 billion, making it the smallest cabinet agency in terms of staff. And unlike some departments with dozens of bureaus and components, the Education Department has only nine major divisions and three deputy under secretaries.

The department's headquarters is less than a mile from the Capitol, in Federal Office Building Number 6. Additional staff are housed in nearby office buildings. The department also has regional offices in Boston, New York, Philadelphia, Atlanta, Chicago, Dallas, Kansas City, Denver, San Francisco, and Seattle.

All of the department's branches report to the secretary of education, who is appointed by the president with the advice and consent of the Senate. As a cabinet member, the secretary is the president's chief advisor on educational issues. As head of the department, he or she coordinates department operations at headquarters and at regional offices directed by regional representatives.

Under William Bennett's leadership, the department encouraged schools to emphasize the fundamentals of learning—reading, writing, and arithmetic.

At headquarters, the under secretary of education assists the secretary. Also a presidential appointee, the under secretary serves as the department's major policy advisor and manages its daily operations. During the secretary's absence, the under secretary acts as secretary.

The under secretary supervises three offices, each headed by a deputy under secretary. The first, the Office of Management, administers the department's grants, issues contracts, and manages personnel matters. The second, the Office of Planning, Budget, and Evaluation, develops and manages the department's budget, conducts long-range departmental planning, and helps develop the department's legislative program. Finally, the Office of Intergovernmental and Interagency Affairs informs state and local authorities about proposed regulations and guidelines, advises the president and secretary of education about the effect of federal education programs at the state and local levels, and develops educational programs for federal employees. A total of 800 employees work in these three offices.

The Major Components

Nine principal operating components perform the department's major functions. These components are the Office of Legislation, the Office of the General Counsel, the Office of Civil Rights, the Office of Educational Research and Improvement, the Office of Special Education and Rehabilitative Services, the Office of Bilingual Education and Minority Languages Affairs, the Office of Elementary and Secondary Education, the Office of Vocational and Adult Education, and the Office of Postsecondary Education. A presidentially appointed director or assistant secretary heads each component, and each office has its own budget and specialized staff.

The Office of Legislation (OL) helps formulate education legislation by informing Congress of the department's activities and

The Department of
Education Organization

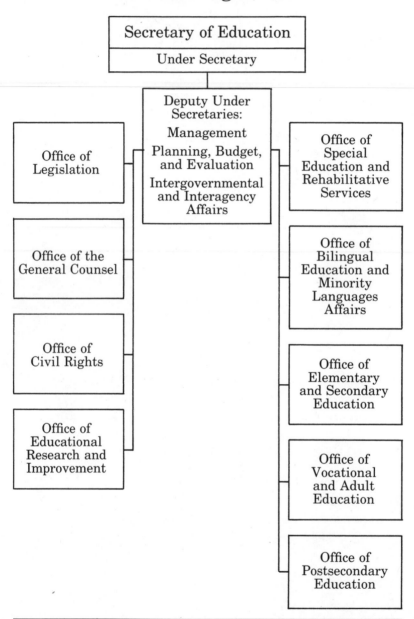

Secretary of Education

Under Secretary

Deputy Under Secretaries:

Management

Planning, Budget, and Evaluation

Intergovernmental and Interagency Affairs

Office of Legislation

Office of the General Counsel

Office of Civil Rights

Office of Educational Research and Improvement

Office of Special Education and Rehabilitative Services

Office of Bilingual Education and Minority Languages Affairs

Office of Elementary and Secondary Education

Office of Vocational and Adult Education

Office of Postsecondary Education

proposing bills for educational reform. The office's Legislative Reference Unit maintains archives of legislative materials on federal education programs.

The Office of the General Counsel (OGC), headed by the presidentially appointed general counsel, is staffed largely by lawyers. It provides legal services to the secretary and other department officials and helps draft and review regulations. It also provides legal advice on proposed education legislation.

One of the department's most active components, the Office of Civil Rights (OCR), enforces federal statutes against discrimination in federally funded education programs. Although the OCR

Students eating lunch in a desegregated school. The Office of Civil Rights, one of the Education Department's nine major components, monitors schools' compliance with federal antidiscrimination laws.

seeks voluntary compliance with federal laws, it can refuse to fund programs that violate federal antidiscrimination laws.

The Office of Educational Research and Improvement (OERI) collects statistics, researches educational issues, and attempts to improve educational techniques by distributing its findings to educators and to the public at large. The OERI's five divisions, each headed by a director, are the Office of Research, the Center for Statistics, Programs for the Improvement of Practice, Information Services, and Library Programs.

Education and rehabilitation programs for handicapped and disabled youths and adults fall under the control of the Office of Special Education and Rehabilitative Services (OSERS). The office's annual budget of more than $2.6 billion funds three major divisions: the Office of Special Education Programs, the Rehabilitation Services Administration, and the National Institute of Handicapped Research.

The Education Department's Office of Special Education and Rehabilitative Services develops programs for youths such as this handicapped student, shown using a specially designed typewriter.

Education Department funds help ensure that students receive equal opportunities, regardless of sex, race, or national origin.

The Office of Bilingual Education and Minority Languages Affairs (OBEMLA) administers programs authorized by the Bilingual Education Act, the Emergency Immigrant Education Act of 1984, and the Transitional Program for Refugee Children. These programs provide aid and guidelines for bilingual education and other programs in schools with large numbers of minority-language-speaking and immigrant students.

The department's second-largest division, the Office of Elementary and Secondary Education (OESE), has a staff of 257 and an annual budget of more than $5 billion. It manages a huge slate of congressionally mandated programs that provide financial assistance to public and private schools. Its programs fall into four

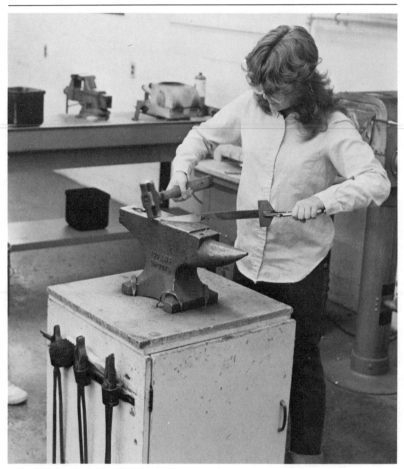

The Education Department's Office of Vocational and Adult Education (OVAE) funds programs that train students for various trades, including metalworking.

categories: compensatory education (remedial instruction for socially and economically deprived students), state and local education, migrant education, and finally, Native American (Indian) education. A separate OESE unit monitors programs in each of these categories.

Almost 20 million Americans are enrolled in programs run by the Office of Vocational and Adult Education (OVAE), which administers grants, contracts, and technical assistance programs. OVAE-funded programs offer career training in the fields of agriculture, health care, occupational home economics, business, technology, trade and industry, and commercial distribution. The office has three divisions: vocational education, adult education, and program innovation and development.

The Office of Postsecondary Education (OPE) distributes almost half of the Department of Education's yearly budget. Each year, the OPE grants more than $9 billion in aid to individual students and to institutions of higher learning. The office's major program units include the Office of Student Financial Assistance, which administers aid programs; the Office of Higher Education Programs, which provides financial aid to institutions of higher education; and the Fund for the Improvement of Postsecondary Education, which finances innovative projects in such areas as teacher education and curriculum development.

OVAE provides funds not only for vocational training, but for adult education classes such as the one pictured here.

The department's various offices often interact. For example, each office uses the data collected by the Office of Educational Research and Improvement. And the Office of Legislation maintains contact with the other offices to help it formulate relevant legislation. Fortunately, the department's small size makes it easy for staff members from different offices to communicate with one another.

Education and Congress

The Department of Education works closely with Congress. Because one of the department's chief duties is administering education legislation, Congress takes an interest in every facet of the department's operations. It manages the department's budget and carefully examines the way the department issues aid-to-education grants.

Both houses of Congress have committees and subcommittees that draft legislation concerning education. The department's Office of Legislation works closely with these committees to help create laws that will benefit the American educational system.

Department officials must appear regularly before Congress. Congressional committees frequently call on the secretary of education to testify and on certain assistant secretaries to report their progress and problems. For example, the assistant secretary for civil rights reports annually on the status of equal opportunity in America's schools.

State Education Departments

Since most educational control rests with the states, each state has its own education department. These state agencies interact with the federal department in many ways. For example, although the department awards some federal grants directly to institutions or individuals, it distributes others—known as *formula* grants—to state education departments for allocation to programs that meet federal guidelines.

State education departments must report to the federal Department of Education on a regular basis. They must tell how they used federal money and must regularly report their general educational findings and activities. However, state agencies enjoy a great deal of autonomy in directing their educational activities. In addition to federal funds, state education departments also receive funds from their own governments to distribute according to the state legislatures.

In carrying out its primary mission, educational research, the Education Department studies new ways to aid handicapped children.

SEVEN

The Department's Mission

Since the federal education agency was founded in 1867 its primary activity has been educational research. Today, the Department of Education uses its research for a variety of purposes. It not only informs educators, legislators, and the public of educational trends, but also administers grants, develops programs, and provides a variety of services that aid the federal education effort.

Each of the department's nine components is devoted to a particular aspect of educational research. Some analyze American academic achievement, some survey educational techniques, and others assess special programs designed to aid minorities and the handicapped. The component that conducts the most research is the Office of Educational Research and Improvement (OERI).

The OERI uses 11 independent educational research and development centers, each assigned to focus on a particular topic relating to American education. Subjects include teacher quality and effectiveness, student testing, and the relationship between

75

Researching employment patterns helps the Education Department develop useful job-training programs, such as this construction class.

education and employment. The OERI also conducts national tests that assess the scholastic achievement of 9-, 13-, and 17-year-old students and compare the results to those of students in other nations.

Other offices also conduct research. For example, the Office of Civil Rights studies civil rights issues and surveys the participation of minorities and women in federally assisted programs. And the Office of Special Education and Rehabilitative Services funds research on methods of educating handicapped people.

Publications

The department publishes much of its research for distribution to legislators, educators, and the general public. In fact, it issues hundreds of pamphlets, books, and papers on its findings. One of its best-known publications is *American Education Magazine*, published monthly. The magazine reports the results of Department of Education studies and outlines new programs and funding opportunities so that educators can apply for available grants.

Once a year, the OERI publishes *The Condition of Education*. This publication includes statistics from states, other federal

To publicize the results of its research projects, the Education Department issues hundreds of publications.

agencies, and private institutions that reveal the nation's educational needs, strengths, and potential problems.

In addition to these publications, the department issues a variety of specialized studies and reports. One regularly updated publication, *Class of '72*, deals with the educational and vocational histories of a sample group of 22,000 people who were high school seniors in 1972. Other specialized publications include the *Educational Directory: Colleges and Universities*, which surveys the nation's institutions of higher learning, and *Access America*, which helps handicapped people file complaints against federal buildings that do not comply with handicapped access standards.

Funding

The majority of the department's budget goes toward funding local educational projects. And the department spends much of its time researching what projects should be funded and which states or local districts need funds. For example, the Office of Bilingual Education and Minority Languages Affairs (OBEMLA) surveys the number of minority language students in each region of the country and provides funds to schools that need minority-language courses.

Another example of combined research and funding is the department's Migrant Education Program. The Office of Migrant Education identifies the children of migrant workers (farm workers who travel the country in search of jobs) and keeps a data bank of education and health information on them. This helps the department distribute funds for tutoring and health services. In 1986, it granted almost $250 million in aid for migrant education programs.

Another aspect of funding is ensuring that state and local school authorities abide by federal laws regarding education. The department does this by awarding grants to schools that comply with federal guidelines and by denying grants to schools that do

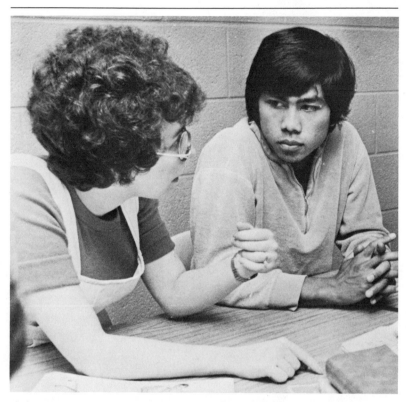

A foreign-born student (right) learns English. The Department of Education oversees bilingual education in the nation's schools.

not. For example, OBEMLA reviews school districts that have large numbers of minority-language students. Those districts that abide by federal bilingual education regulations are eligible for federal aid to support language training, acculturation (adaptation to a new culture), and special guidance counselors for the students.

Project Development

In addition to funding projects that localities propose, the Department of Education also uses its research to develop new projects. The OERI operates nine regional laboratories that de-

The Education Department's researchers develop new educational programs, many of which involve computer training.

velop programs to improve education techniques. These laboratories do not conduct original research. Rather, they use the research conducted by other units of the department or by state or private agencies to promote exemplary education programs.

In the past, OERI provided funding to develop public educational television series, such as "Sesame Street" and "3-2-1 Contact." Today, some of its programs emphasize technological skills, such as computer training.

Another project development effort is the Women's Education Equity Act Program, administered by the Office of Elementary and Secondary Education (OESE). This program awards grants to individuals, schools, colleges and universities, and private institutions to develop programs for or about women.

The Office of Educational Research and Improvement has funded many public-television programs, such as Sesame Street.

Other Services

Many of the department's divisions also provide or fund other services. For example, the Information Services unit of OERI operates the Educational Research Library in Washington, D.C., which contains an extensive collection of educational materials—180,000 books, as well as microfilms, newspapers, and periodicals. The library, which is open to the public, includes a noted collection of rare educational books, including many published before 1800.

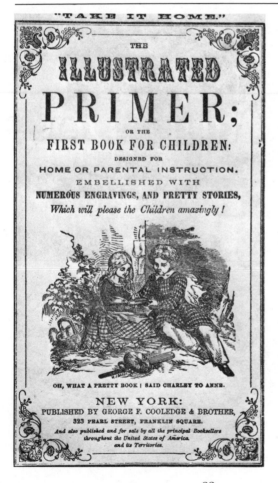

A 19th-century advertisement for a primer. The Education Department's library houses such rare books, as well as modern documents.

Information Services also operates the Educational Resources Information Center (ERIC), a computerized library of more than 500,000 documents on education. Some libraries are equipped with terminals that can tap into ERIC; other libraries and the general public can receive ERIC information on microfiche. ERIC is continually updated with recent findings, making it the most complete source of educational material in the country.

Other services enable college and public libraries to build facilities, buy books and equipment, tie into ERIC, and conduct other activities. Department specialists also advise librarians and state education officials on library matters.

In addition to these library services, the department also provides training and education services for its members and other government employees. For example, the Office of Management operates the Horace Mann Learning Center. Named for America's most famous 19th-century educator, the Mann Center provides training for the Department of Education staff.

Each of these functions serves the same goal: to improve education in America. By studying educational trends, encouraging innovative programs, and increasing awareness of education techniques and problems, the Department of Education attempts to guide the nation's schools without infringing on the rights of states, localities, institutions, and individuals to direct their own academic affairs.

Students learn to program computers. A major goal of the Education Department is to help students succeed in an increasingly technological world.

EIGHT

The Educational Outlook

The Department of Education, the youngest and smallest of the cabinet departments, faces one of the greatest challenges of any federal agency. Although the American people want their government to support education, they balk at too much federal control. At a time when American education is in dire need of improvement, the department must walk the fine line between the public's approval of some federal involvement in education and its fear of "big government".

Recent studies have shown that American students score consistently lower on standardized academic tests than do students in many other industrialized nations. The world leaders in academic testing, the Japanese, score more than 15 percent higher than Americans do in math tests. Algebra and calculus scores among America's top high school seniors are lower than those of students in any other Western country.

Studies have also revealed that 20 million American adults are functionally illiterate—they cannot read and write well enough to fill out a job application or choose a box of cereal in the grocery store. This number is increasing daily as high schools grant diplomas to students who cannot read and as non-English-speaking immigrants pour into the country.

The influx of immigrants and the recent rise in the number of children entering have also led to overcrowding in some school districts. In some areas of the country, schools have adopted 12-month schedules so that school buildings that usually sit idle all summer can be used year-round. Under this system, students go to school for three months at a time, then have a month off, repeating the pattern for one year until they advance to the next grade level. Parents and students have protested against this concept and the problems that come with it: disruption of family vacations, off-months interfering with participation in sports and extracurricular activities, and the difficulties of learning in a classroom made stifling by summer heat.

Adding to the country's educational problems is the fact that parental involvement in education has slackened; many students

Students practice their writing skills. Under President Reagan, the Education Department encouraged schools to place renewed emphasis on writing after studies revealed that an alarming number of Americans were functionally illiterate.

receive no encouragement in the home to perform at school. Moreover, other activities, most notably sports, have replaced academics as the way to achieve success in the school environment. Coaches and school officials often look the other way as high school and college athletes ignore their academic courses to concentrate on sports.

As American industry becomes more technological and service-oriented, basic skills such as reading, writing, mathematics, and logic will be more important to the economic success of individuals and the country as a whole. The nation has already suffered from foreign competition in the economic sphere, most of it from Japan—the country with the highest academic test scores.

The Department of Education is aware of these problems. In its 1986 report, *What Works*, the department examined declining academic achievement and recommended ways to improve American education. The report stressed parental involvement, discipline, and a return to basic educational techniques—phonetic reading, hands-on training, and emphasizing the value of working hard to achieve academic success.

Perhaps the report's most important finding was that students achieve academically only when they understand the value of a sound education. "Children who . . . attach importance to education," the report noted, "are likely to have higher academic achievement and fewer disciplinary problems than those who do not."

Although ambivalence has characterized the federal government's education policy throughout the nation's history, plans to abolish the Department of Education remain unfulfilled. Today, education programs are supported by powerful groups who urge the government to act to improve education. The Department of Education seems likely to persevere as Americans increasingly recognize that the nation's very survival may depend upon education.

GLOSSARY

Bilingual education – Teaching minority-language students both in their native language and in English.

Busing – Transportation of students to schools outside their areas of residence as a means of accomplishing desegregation.

Civil rights – The rights of personal liberty and equal treatment guaranteed to all Americans by the Constitution and various civil-rights laws.

Curriculum – A school's educational program.

Desegregation – Eliminating the voluntary or enforced isolation of races in separate schools or living areas.

Formula grants – Department of Education grants distributed to schools by state education departments.

Illiteracy – The inability to read or write.

National Education Association (NEA) – The largest and most powerful teachers' union in the United States.

New Deal – A slate of federal programs instituted by American president Franklin D. Roosevelt during the 1930s to promote economic recovery.

Phonetic reading – A system of reading in which students sound out words syllable by syllable.

Postsecondary education – Education beyond the high-school level.

Progressive education – An educational system that emphasizes life skills, such as home economics and physical education, rather than traditional academics.

Sexism – Prejudice or discriminatory behavior against one gender.

Special education – Educational programs for students with learning disabilities, physical handicaps, or emotional problems.

Vocational education – Education aimed at training people for technical occupations and trades.

SELECTED REFERENCES

Graham, Hugh Davis. *The Uncertain Triumph: Federal Education Policy in the Kennedy and Johnson Years.* Chapel Hill: The University of North Carolina Press, 1984.

Kursch, Harry. *The United States Office of Education: A Century of Service.* Philadelphia: Chilton Books, 1965.

Ravitch, Diane. *The Troubled Crusade: American Education, 1945–1980.* New York: Basic Books, 1983.

Sproull, Lee, Stephen Weiner, and David Wolf. *Organizing an Anarchy: Belief, Bureaucracy, and Politics in the National Institute of Education.* Chicago: University of Chicago Press, 1978.

Stein, Harold, ed. The Office of Education Library. *In Public Administration and Policy Development: A Case Book.* New York: Harcourt, Brace & World, 1948.

Tiedt, Sidney W. *The Role of the Federal Government in Education.* New York: Oxford University Press, 1966.

Warren, Donald R. *To Enforce Education: A History of the Founding Years of the United States Office of Education.* Detroit: Wayne State University Press, 1974.

INDEX

Office of Postsecondary
Education (OPE), 65, 71
Office of Special Education and
Rehabilitative Services
(OSERS), 65, 76
Office of Vocational and Adult
Education (OVAE), 70–71

P
private education, 60, 69
progressive education, 35
public education, 17, 18, 23, 24,
51, 69

R
Reagan, Ronald, 57, 61
Rhode Island, 24
Roosevelt, Franklin D., 41

S
Scholastic Aptitude Test (SAT),
51
school prayer, 18
segregation, 18, 50
Senate, U.S., 26, 54, 55, 56, 64
sex education, 18
sexism, 50
Studebaker, John Ward, 41, 42,
43
Supreme Court, 50

T
Taft, William Howard, 37
Tennessee, 33
Tigert, John James, 39
Transitional Program for Refugee
Children, 69

U
United States Garden Army
Project, 38
University of Alabama, 34
University of Geneva, 21

V
vocational training, 38, 41

W
War on Poverty, 47
Washington, George, 21–22
What Works, 60, 87
Women's Educational Equity Act,
50
Works Progress Administration,
41
World War I, 38, 41
World War II, 43

Y
Yale University, 24

Stephen J. Sniegoski is a historian for the U.S. Department of Education in Washington, D.C. He holds a Ph.D. from the University of Maryland and has published many articles and essays in magazines and scholarly journals.

Arthur M. Schlesinger, jr., served in the White House as special assistant to Presidents Kennedy and Johnson. He is the author of numerous acclaimed works in American history and has twice been awarded the Pulitzer Prize. He taught history at Harvard College for many years and is currently Albert Schweitzer Professor of the Humanities at the City College of New York.